# READING LINK

## WORKBOOK 1 – DECODING

Carol A. Christensen

**L** iteracy
**I** deas
**N** europrocesses
**K** nowledge

For more information, please visit
www.kbs.com – the Americas
www.kbs.co.uk – UK/Europe
www.kbs.com.au – Asia/Pacific

Acknowledgements
Publisher Rob Watts
Graphics Dean Maynard



Knowledge Books and Software
ABN 75003053316
Unit 4/498 Scottsdale Drive, Varsity Lakes,
Queensland, 4227, Australia
Telephone: (07) 5568 0288
Facsimile: (07) 5568 0277
Email: orders@kbs.com.au
Website: www.kbs.com.au

Printed in China

ISBN: 1920824 86-3

Product code: E041

# Contents

# Conditions of Purchase

1. Photocopying of any part of this book for any purpose is strictly forbidden without prior permission from the publisher.
2. You must use a **LINK – Decoding** registered and accredited instructor/teacher with this book. The process and instruction techniques must be followed precisely to be effective in improving reading.

For further details, please contact the publisher.

# Instructions for Teachers

This workbook is designed for children who are in the earliest stages of learning to read. It is also suitable for older students experiencing difficulty in learning to read (see **LINK Decoding Assessment**).

The aim of the program is to provide students with a carefully structured and sequenced program to develop their ability to decode written text. The activities in this workbook are designed to enable students to use letter-sound correspondences to work out unfamiliar words. There are also sight words for students to learn and activities that establish the foundation for comprehension.

## Decoding skills

Teachers should refer to the **Teacher's Manual** before commencing the program. For each lesson you will need the large letter cards listed at the base of each page. Separate the letters to be introduced from all the other letters.

Each lesson follows the same series of steps:

Step 1: Using the large letter cards, introduce the sound of each new letter. The letters that need to be introduced are listed at the bottom of each page. Tell the students the sound that the letter makes. **Do not use letter names**. For example, for the letter '*s*', tell the students that this letter makes the sound '*sss*'. Practise the letter-sound correspondence a few times.

Step 2: Think of words that begin and end with the sound of each new letter; for example, '*sun*' begins with '*sss*' and '*house*' ends with the sound '*sss*'.

Step 3: Display the letters of the first word; for example, for the word '*sat*' display '*s*' '*a*' and '*t*'.

Step 4: This step teaches students to use their letter-sounds to work out unfamiliar words. It is the most important step in the sequence. Help the students sound out the word that has been displayed. Say the sounds of each letter, and then repeat them getting faster and faster and blending them together until the students can say the word. Try not to actually say the word but blend the letters so quickly that the students can recognise the word.

Step 5: After students identify the word, they should use the word in a sentence.

Step 6: Repeat steps 3-5 for each word in the list.

Step 7: When all the words have been introduced, students should practise reading the words in the workbook. **Read across the page.** The aim of this step is to facilitate students' ability to use their letter-sounds to work out words. It provides extended practice in working out the words. You should repeat the process of reading the words in the workbook until the students are fast, accurate and efficient at reading the words.

**Accuracy is essential.** Do not allow students to continue through the words if they make an error. When an error occurs, you should wait until they can work out the correct word. They should be 100% accurate.

It is not intended that students learn the words as sight words. The focus should always be on using the letter-sounds to work out the words.

Step 8: When students are proficient at reading the words, they should spell each word on the spelling sheet. Make sure that any errors they make are corrected.

Step 9: When students have developed some proficiency in reading the list, they can complete a time trial at the end of each module. Students can do as many time trials as they would like until they reach criterion. They should graph each attempt at the time trial. Graphing their improvement leads to high levels of motivation as they see their improvement. When they reach criterion, they can move on to the next list of words.

This sequence of steps should be used for all lists in the workbook.

## Time trials

Mastery tests can be strong motivators. For each list of words, read the words in the workbook. When the students are ready, **see how many words they can read in 45 seconds**. Write the number of the list in the last row.

Students can mark and colour the number of words they read in each time trial on the graph. Students may take a time trial on each list as many times as necessary. The goal of each time trial is for the student to read one more word in the set time than they did on the previous attempt.

Recognise students in some way each time they increase the number of words they read in a time trial; for example, they could be given a stamp or sticker.

**Criterion to progress to the next list** of words is marked on each graph – 48 words in 45 seconds. When students reach criterion, they should receive a 'special' reward. Public recognition for achievement is a powerful reward; for example, as students reach criterion, they could stand while the class applauds them.

**Ensure that each student works to his or her ability.** Comparing performance between students can have strong negative effects. Recognition should be made when a student masters a list of words, rather than if he or she does better than other students in the class. This encourages all students to strive to reach their potential, rather than a single student being the 'best'.

# MODULE 1

## Consonant-Vowel-Consonant Words

# Overview of Module 1

| Section | Words | Letters introduced | | | Letters used | |
|---|---|---|---|---|---|---|
| | | Vowels | Consonants | | Vowels | Consonants |
| | | | Initial | Final | | |
| List 1 | sat<br>met<br>rat<br>set | a e | s m r | _t | a e | s m r t |
| List 2 | mat<br>sap<br>pet<br>tap | | p t | _p | a e | m s p t |
| List 3 | pat<br>map<br>pep<br>cat | | c | | a e | m c p t |
| Review 1 | sat<br>sap<br>met<br>cat<br>tap<br>pat<br>pep<br>set<br>mat<br>rat | | | | | |
| List 4 | ted<br>pit<br>dad<br>rid | i | d | _d | a e i | p r t d |
| List 5 | sit<br>red<br>did<br>get | | g | | e i | g s r d t |
| List 6 | fat<br>rip<br>fed<br>gap | | f | | a e i | f r g t d p |
| Review 2 | dad<br>rip<br>sit<br>ted<br>pit<br>rid<br>red<br>fat<br>gap<br>did<br>get<br>fed | | | | | |

| Section | Words | Letters introduced | | | Letters used | |
|---|---|---|---|---|---|---|
| | | Vowels | Consonants | | Vowels | Consonants |
| | | | Initial | Final | | |
| List 7 | hat<br>fit<br>rod<br>had<br>got | o | h | | a i o | h f r g t d |
| List 8 | sip<br>leg<br>hid<br>pod<br>mad | | l | _g | a e i o | s l h m p<br>g d |
| List 9 | cot<br>wet<br>sad<br>pig<br>mud | u | w | | a e i<br>o u | c w s m d<br>t p g |
| List 10 | **Sight words**<br>the<br>little<br>go<br>so<br>no | | | | | |
| Review 3 | got<br>sip<br>leg<br>the<br>cot<br>go<br>fit<br>had<br>little<br>sad<br>mad<br>hid | | | | | |

| | | | | |
|---|---|---|---|---|
| sat | met | rat | set | sat |
| met | set | sat | met | rat |
| rat | sat | set | rat | met |
| rat | set | met | rat | sat |
| sat | met | rat | sat | set |
| met | set | sat | met | rat |
| set | sat | set | rat | met |
| rat | set | sat | met | sat |

Letters introduced in this list: **a e s m r _t**
All letters used in this list: **a e s m r t**
Follow the directions on **Page 1**.

## Any mistakes?

After they read the words, students should spell each word in the list. If they make an error, the correct word should be written in the first column below the line. Students should copy the word three times, cover it over and then test themselves. Use another sheet of paper if students need more practice. If students seem to make a number of errors, or if they seem to be unable to remember how to spell a particular word, check the **Problem Solver** section of the **Teacher's Manual** for suggestions on how to address spelling problems. Do not continue to the next list until each student can spell all words correctly.

| | | | | |
|---|---|---|---|---|
| mat | pet | sap | tap | mat |
| pet | tap | mat | pet | sap |
| sap | mat | tap | sap | pet |
| sap | tap | pet | sap | mat |
| mat | tap | sap | mat | pet |
| tap | pet | mat | tap | sap |
| pet | mat | pet | sap | tap |
| sap | pet | mat | tap | mat |

Letters introduced in this list: **p _p**

All letters used in this list: **a e m s t p**

Repeat the steps as in **List 1**.

**TIP:** When practising words in the workbook, the goal is for students to become fast and accurate at using their letter-sounds to work out unfamiliar words. The goal is not for students to learn the words as 'sight words'.

## Any mistakes?

| | | | | |
|---|---|---|---|---|
| map | pat | pep | cat | map |
| pat | cat | map | pat | pep |
| pep | map | cat | pep | pat |
| map | cat | pat | map | pep |
| pep | pat | map | pep | cat |
| pat | cat | pep | pat | map |
| cat | pep | cat | map | pat |
| map | cat | pep | pat | pep |

Letters introduced in this list: **c**

All letters used in this list: **a e c m p p t**

**TIP:** When students can read the words on the page fairly well, remember to do the time trial at the end of this module. Students must master of all the words in each module before continuing on to the next module.

## Any mistakes?

| | | | | |
|---|---|---|---|---|
| sat | met | sap | met | cat |
| tap | pat | pep | set | mat |
| map | rat | tap | pat | pep |
| met | sat | met | sap | set |
| sap | cat | sap | met | met |
| met | tap | met | cat | sat |
| cat | pat | sat | tap | rat |
| tap | pep | rat | pat | set |

**NOTE:** In review lessons:

1. Revise the letter-sounds for the previous three lists.
2. Read the words in the workbook going across the page.
3. When students feel ready, complete the time trial.

# PUZZLE 1: Word-picture match

rat 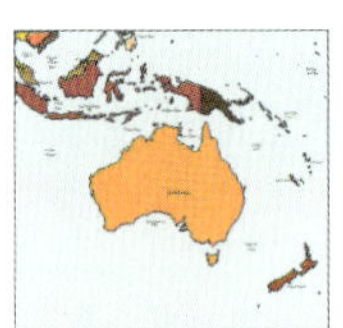

met 

map 

cat 

mat 

pat 

tap 

Read the words. Find the picture that matches each word. Draw a line from the word to the matching picture.

| | | | | |
|---|---|---|---|---|
| ted | dad | pit | rid | ted |
| dad | rid | ted | dad | pit |
| pit | ted | rid | pit | dad |
| pit | rid | dad | pit | ted |
| ted | dad | pit | ted | rid |
| rid | dad | ted | rid | pit |
| dad | ted | dad | pit | rid |
| pit | dad | ted | rid | ted |

Letters introduced in this list: **i d _d**
All letters used in this list: **a e i r d p t d**

## Any mistakes?

| | | | | |
|---|---|---|---|---|
| get | sit | did | red | get |
| sit | red | get | sit | did |
| did | get | red | did | sit |
| did | get | sit | did | red |
| did | sit | red | did | get |
| sit | get | did | sit | red |
| get | did | get | red | sit |
| red | get | did | sit | did |

Letters introduced in this list: **g**

All letters used in this list: **e i g s r d t d**

**TIP:** Make sure that you complete the time trial at the end of the module. Do not continue to the next list until every student has reached criterion on the time trial.

## Any mistakes?

| | | | | |
|---|---|---|---|---|
| rip | fed | gap | fat | rip |
| fed | fat | rip | fed | gap |
| fat | rip | gap | fat | fed |
| fat | gap | fed | fat | rip |
| rip | fed | fat | rip | gap |
| fed | fat | rip | fed | gap |
| fat | rip | fat | gap | fed |
| gap | fat | rip | fed | rip |

Letters introduced in this list: **f**

All letters used in this list: **a e i f r g d p t**

**TIP:** Use the time trial at the end of this module to check for mastery. If a student makes an error while doing the time trial, simply point to the word and wait for the student to work out what the word says. The time penalty that occurs when waiting for the correct word will encourage accuracy.

## Any mistakes?

Remember it's important for students to master each list before they move on to the next. If they make an error, the correct word should be written in the first column below the line. Students should copy the word three times, cover it over and then test themselves. Use another sheet of paper, if students need more practice.

| | | | | |
|---|---|---|---|---|
| sit | dad | rip | ted | pit |
| get | fed | dad | did | rid |
| sit | ted | rip | gap | red |
| get | pit | fed | dad | fat |
| fed | rid | fat | red | gap |
| did | red | gap | rid | did |
| gap | fat | did | pit | get |
| fat | gap | get | dad | fed |

**TIP:** Remember to read the words across the page. Place a ruler or piece of paper under each line to help students focus on the correct line to read.

| | | | | | | | | | |
|---|---|---|---|---|---|---|---|---|---|
| s | t | e | d | m | a | t | g | e | t |
| d | a | d | a | r | i | p | i | t | m |
| c | s | a | p | i | t | a | g | d | a |
| p | r | i | d | p | e | t | f | a | t |
| t | i | p | r | e | d | i | d | d | f |
| m | p | i | f | a | t | f | e | d | a |
| s | r | d | a | d | d | e | g | e | t |
| g | e | t | t | r | e | d | a | s | e |
| f | a | t | s | i | g | a | p | i | d |
| s | t | g | a | p | f | g | e | t | m |

**ted pit dad rid sit red**

**did get fat rip fed gap**

Ask students to find the words above. They can colour each letter square that is part of a word in the puzzle. Words could be coloured a different colour. Students should count the number of times they can find each word. Then see if they can find any other words. Words are arranged horizontally (across), vertically (down) or diagonally.

| | | | | |
|---|---|---|---|---|
| hat | fit | got | had | rod |
| fit | rod | got | fit | hat |
| got | hat | fit | rod | fit |
| rod | had | had | got | hat |
| hat | fit | got | hat | had |
| fit | had | rod | hat | got |
| rod | hat | got | had | fit |
| got | had | rod | fit | hat |

Letters introduced in this list: **o h**

All letters used in this list: **a i o h f r g t d**

**TIP:** Make sure you provide cues, hints and assistance so that students easily work out every word. However, do not tell students the word – allow them to work it out.

## Any mistakes?

| | | | | |
|---|---|---|---|---|
| sip | hid | mad | leg | pod |
| hid | leg | sip | pod | mad |
| pod | sip | leg | mad | hid |
| mad | leg | hid | mad | sip |
| sip | hid | rod | sip | leg |
| hid | leg | sip | rod | mad |
| rod | sip | leg | mad | hid |
| mad | leg | sip | hid | sip |

Letters introduced in this list: **l _g**
All letters used in this list: **a e i o s l h m p g d**

## Any mistakes?

| | | | | |
|---|---|---|---|---|
| mud | wet | sad | cot | pig |
| pig | cot | mud | wet | sad |
| sad | mud | cot | pig | wet |
| sad | cot | pig | sad | mud |
| pig | wet | sad | mud | cot |
| mud | cot | pig | sad | wet |
| cot | pig | mud | wet | sad |
| wet | cot | pig | sad | pig |

Letters introduced in this list: **u w**

All letters used in this list: **a e i o u  c w s m g d p t**

**TIP:** Check the problem solver section of the **Teacher's Manual** for help when working with students who seem to have difficulty in making progress.

## Any mistakes?

# You are a star!

You have reached **List 10** of
**Module 1** of **LINK – Decoding**

# MODULE 1 LIST 10: Sight Words – Instructions

**Step 1**: Tell students that many words can be worked out using letter sounds but some words cannot be worked out. We have to learn them as whole words.

**Step 2**: Tell students that these words have a particular name. (For older students you can call them 'sight words'; however, for younger students, it's better to give them a name that will act as a trigger for memory, for example, 'tricky words', or 'weird words'.)

**Step 3**: Introduce words one at a time on letter cards. It is important not to use individual letter cards to make the words. This is another way that helps students store these words in memory. As each word is introduced, ask students to use it in a sentence.

**Step 4**: Practise the words on letter cards for a few minutes.

**Step 5**: Students should practise the words by reading them in their workbooks.

**TIP:** Read down the column.

| | | | | |
|---|---|---|---|---|
| the | go | so | no | little |
| go | little | the | so | no |
| no | so | little | no | go |
| so | little | go | no | the |
| go | the | so | no | little |
| the | little | go | so | little |
| little | so | the | go | no |
| the | little | go | so | go |

## Any mistakes?

| | | | | |
|---|---|---|---|---|
| got | sip | leg | the | cot |
| hid | little | fit | sad | go |
| got | had | go | mad | fit |
| sip | leg | fit | hid | had |
| the | sip | cot | sad | little |
| cot | hid | the | mad | sad |
| go | fit | leg | little | mad |
| had | mad | sip | had | hid |

| | | | |
|---|---|---|---|
| h__t | fi__ | l_g | _ip |
| we_ | c_t | _ig | s_d |
| mu_ | h_d | li__le | g_t |

Fill in a letter to make a word. Tell the students to read the words. They can look through their workbook to find some other words that they can make with these letters; write them under the other words.

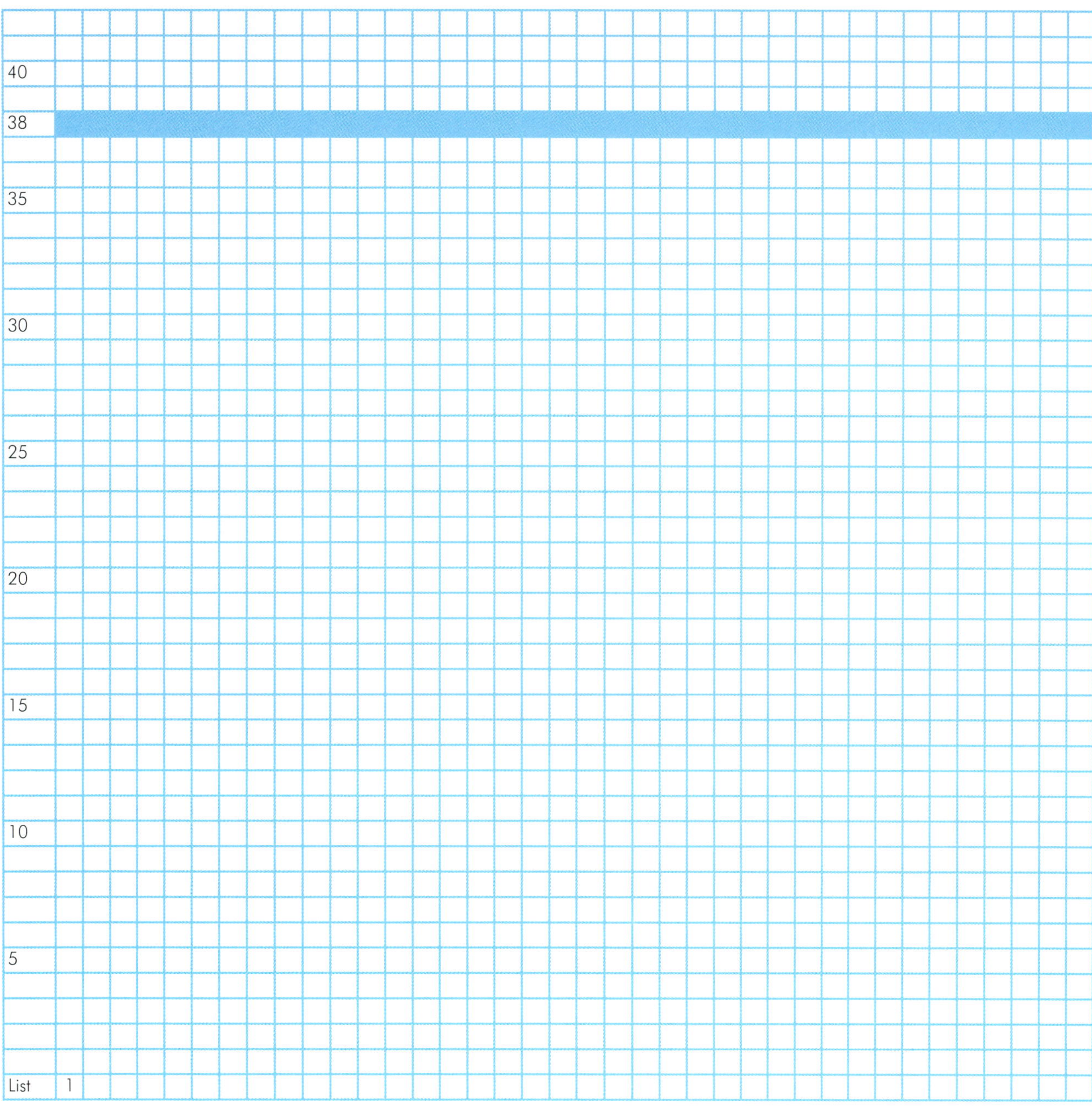


Mastery tests can be strong motivators.

For each list of words, read the words in the workbook. When the students are ready, **see how many words they can read in 45 seconds**. Write the number of the list in the last row.

Students can mark and colour the number of words they read in each time trial on the graph. Students may take a time trial on each list as many times as necessary. The goal of each time trial is for the student to read one more word in the set time than they did on the previous attempt.

Recognise students in some way each time they increase the number of words they read in a time trial; for example, they could be given a stamp or sticker.

**Criterion to progress to the next list of words is marked on the graph** – 38 words in 45 seconds. When students reach criterion, they should receive a 'special' reward. Public recognition for achievement is a powerful reward. For example, as students reach criterion, they could stand while the class applauds them.

**Ensure that each student works to his or her ability.** Comparing performance between students can have strong negative effects. Recognition should be made when a student masters a list of words, rather than if he or she does better than other students. This encourages all students to strive to reach their potential, rather than a single student be the 'best'.

# MODULE 2

## Introducing Initial Consonant Blends

# Overview of Module 2

| Section | Words | Letters introduced | | Letters used | |
|---|---|---|---|---|---|
| | | Consonants | | Vowels | Consonants |
| | | Initial | Final | | |
| List 1 | hot<br>lip<br>top<br>lad<br>trot<br>sod | tr | | a i o | h l s t p d<br>tr |
| List 2 | not<br>lid<br>hop<br>lap<br>stop<br>tag | n<br>st | | a i o | n l h t d p g<br>st |
| List 3 | dot<br>bat<br>cup<br>stag<br>bed<br>nut | b | | a e o u | b c n d t p g<br>st |
| Review 1 | top trot<br>lad bat<br>not hot<br>cup bed<br>stop stag<br>hop lip<br>nut tag | | | | |
| List 4 | pup<br>sled<br>let<br>slab<br>rib<br>hut | sl | _b | a e i u | l r h p d b t<br>sl |
| List 5 | mop<br>clip<br>bad<br>rub<br>slog<br>lot | cl | | a i o u | m b r l p d g t<br>cl sl |
| List 6 | tip<br>but<br>jet<br>clod<br>bit<br>jab | j | | a e i o u | j b t p d<br>cl |

| Section | Words | Letters introduced | | Letters used | |
|---|---|---|---|---|---|
| | | Consonants | | Vowels | Consonants |
| | | Initial | Final | | |
| Review 2 | sit but<br>dad rid<br>bit did<br>ted jet<br>pit red<br>get clod | | | | |
| List 7 | slim<br>jam<br>clap<br>job<br>pot<br>slug<br>kid | k | _m | a i o u | j k m p b t g d<br>sl cl |
| List 8 | bib<br>scat<br>stem<br>slam<br>jot<br>yet<br>clop | y<br>sc | | a e i o | j y b t m p<br>sc st sl cl |
| List 9 | drag<br>yes<br>rig<br>drop<br>jug<br>quit<br>yum | dr<br>qu | _s | a e i o u | y r j g s p t m<br>dr qu |
| List 10 | Sight words<br>I<br>they<br>you<br>one<br>said | | | | |
| Review 3 | jam clop<br>slug drag<br>clap said<br>job quit<br>slim jug<br>scat you<br>bib they<br>slam yum<br>jog one<br>yet stem | | | | |

| | | | | |
|---|---|---|---|---|
| hot | lad | top | lip | trot |
| sod | lip | trot | lad | sod |
| trot | hot | sod | top | lad |
| top | lip | lad | trot | sod |
| sod | trot | top | hot | lip |
| trot | lip | sod | lad | top |
| lip | hot | trot | top | sod |
| top | lip | hot | lad | trot |

Letters introduced in this list: **tr**
All letters used in this list: **a i o tr h l s t p d**

## Any mistakes?

**TIP:** Spelling and decoding involve opposite processes. When decoding, students need to use their letter-sound to work out a word by blending the sounds together. When spelling, students start with a word, and must break (segment) it into sounds. Then they must attach a letter to the sound and write the letter. This is called 'encoding'. Check to see if students who are having difficulty in spelling are breaking the word into sounds. Using letter names rather than letter-sounds can interfere with the encoding process.

| | | | | |
|---|---|---|---|---|
| not | hop | stop | lid | tag |
| lid | tag | not | lap | stop |
| hop | lap | lid | not | tag |
| lap | stop | lid | tag | hop |
| tag | not | stop | lid | lap |
| hop | lap | tag | stop | not |
| lid | stop | not | tag | hop |
| lap | hop | tag | stop | lid |

Letters introduced in this list: **n st**

All letters used in this list: **a i o st n l h t d p g**

**TIP:** When practising words in the workbook, the goal is for students to become fast and accurate at using their letter-sounds to work out words. The goal is not for students to recognise 'sight words'. It is more important that they can use the letters to decode unknown words than it is for them to recognise the particular words in the workbook.

## Any mistakes?

| | | | | |
|---|---|---|---|---|
| nut | bat | bed | cup | stag |
| bat | stag | dot | bed | nut |
| bed | dot | bat | stag | cup |
| stag | cup | dot | nut | bat |
| bed | nut | stag | cup | dot |
| stag | bed | dot | bat | nut |
| dot | bat | nut | bed | cup |
| nut | cup | dot | bat | stag |

Letters introduced in this list: **b**

All letters used in this list: **a e o u st n b c t p g d**

**TIP:** Students often confuse 'b' and 'd'. Check the **Teacher's Manual** for tips on avoiding this confusion. Give students some cues to help remember the difference, for example: *"'**d**' is for '**dog**'. A dog has a tail on the end and so can '**d**',"* or *"'**bbb bat** comes before the **bbb ball**'."*

## Any mistakes?

| | | | | |
|---|---|---|---|---|
| top | lad | not | cup | stop |
| hop | nut | trot | bat | bed |
| stag | lip | tag | hot | top |
| lad | stag | lip | top | lad |
| not | bat | bed | stop | hop |
| cup | trot | tag | hot | bed |
| stop | bat | stag | tag | top |
| hop | nut | stop | lip | trot |

lad

trot

stop

stag

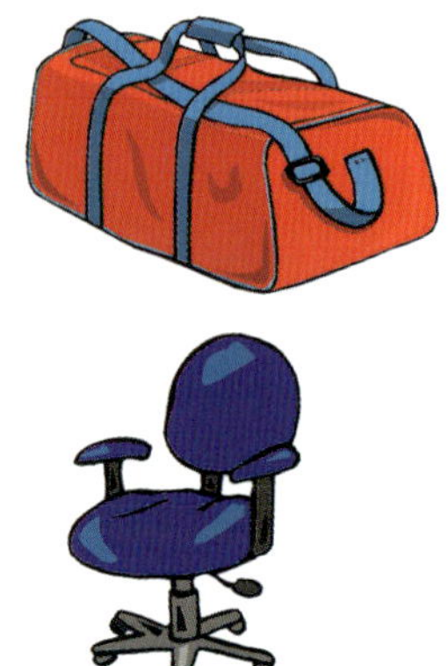

Ask students to read the first word ('**lad**') and name the first two pictures ('**flower**' '**sad**'). They should draw a line between the word '**lad**' and the picture that rhymes with '**lad**'. Repeat these steps for the other words. Pictures are of flower, sad; cot, tree; frog, top; bag, chair.

| | | | | |
|---|---|---|---|---|
| pup | sled | rib | let | slab |
| hut | rib | pup | sled | let |
| sled | hut | slab | rib | hut |
| rib | let | sled | slab | pup |
| slab | pup | let | hut | rib |
| let | slab | rib | sled | hut |
| slab | sled | hut | let | pup |
| pup | rib | slab | hut | sled |

Letters introduced in this list: **sl _b**

All letters used in this list: **a e i u sl l r h p d b t p**

**TIP:** Another trick to remember the difference between '**b**' and '**d**' is to look at the word '**bed**': '**b**' begins '**bed**' and '**d**' comes at the end. The two letters make the head and base boards of the bed.

## Any mistakes?

| | | | | |
|---|---|---|---|---|
| mop | clip | bad | rub | slog |
| lot | bad | clip | rub | mop |
| clip | mop | slog | bad | lot |
| bad | rub | mop | clip | slog |
| slog | clip | lot | mop | clip |
| mop | lot | slog | rub | bad |
| lot | bad | slog | mop | clip |
| clip | mop | bad | slog | rub |

Letters introduced in this list: **cl**

All letters used in this list: **a i o u cl sl m d r l p b t g**

## Any mistakes?

| | | | | |
|---|---|---|---|---|
| bit | but | jet | clod | tip |
| jab | clod | bit | but | jet |
| tip | jab | jet | clod | but |
| clod | jet | tip | clod | bit |
| jab | but | clod | bit | jet |
| tip | clod | bit | but | bit |
| clod | jab | clod | jet | but |
| jet | clod | tip | but | bit |

Letters introduced in this list: j
All letters used in this list: a e i o u cl j b t p d

## Any mistakes?

| | | | | |
|---|---|---|---|---|
| sit | dad | bit | ted | pit |
| get | but | dad | did | rid |
| sit | ted | bit | jet | red |
| get | pit | but | dad | clod |
| but | rid | clod | red | jet |
| did | red | jet | rid | did |
| jet | clod | did | pit | get |
| clod | jet | get | dad | but |

| | | | | | |
|---|---|---|---|---|---|
| l | i | p | u | p | z |
| a | e | e | n | u | t |
| d | s | t | o | p | a |
| c | l | i | p | u | p |
| l | e | t | b | a | d |
| j | d | a | b | b | s |
| e | a | s | l | i | p |
| t | u | b | e | g | a |
| i | n | u | t | i | n |

**lip stop pup clip slip**

**lad nut sled bad jab**

Ask the students to find the words above. See if they can find any other words. They can colour each letter square that is part of a word in the puzzle. Words could be coloured a different colour. Words are arranged horizontally (across), vertically (down) or diagonally.

| | | | | |
|---|---|---|---|---|
| slim | jam | clap | job | pot |
| slug | kid | pot | slim | clap |
| job | clap | slim | jam | slug |
| slug | job | kid | clap | pot |
| slim | clap | jam | pot | kid |
| pot | slug | clap | job | slim |
| clap | job | slim | pot | jam |
| slim | kid | jam | job | slug |

Letters introduced in this list: **k _m**
All letters used in this list: **a i o u sl cl j k p m b t g d**

## Any mistakes?

| | | | | |
|---|---|---|---|---|
| scat | yet | clop | stem | job |
| clop | bib | scat | jot | stem |
| bib | scat | yet | slam | jot |
| yet | scat | jot | clop | slam |
| stem | clop | bib | scat | yet |
| slam | yet | clop | stem | bib |
| slam | jot | scat | yet | clop |
| bib | scat | stem | jot | slam |

Letters introduced in this list: **y sc**

All letters used in this list: **a e i o sc st sl cl j y b t m p b**

**TIP:** Ensure that each student has mastered reading each list before continuing to the next one. Check mastery with the time trial at the end of each module.

## Any mistakes?

| | | | | |
|---|---|---|---|---|
| drag | yes | rig | jug | quit |
| yum | drag | drop | rig | jug |
| yes | rig | quit | drop | yum |
| jug | yes | drag | quit | rig |
| quit | drop | rig | drag | jug |
| drop | jug | yum | yes | quit |
| yum | drop | drag | drop | rig |
| yes | drag | jug | quit | drop |

Letters introduced in this list: **qu dr _s**

All letters used in this list: **a e i o u qu dr y r j g s p t m**

**TIP:** Ensure that students have mastered every word on the list before they move on to the next one. Use the mastery test at the end of the module to ensure that they are ready to proceed to the next list.

## Any mistakes?

| | | | | |
|---|---|---|---|---|
| they | I | one | said | you |
| they | said | I | you | one |
| they | you | one | I | said |
| you | one | said | one | they |
| I | they | you | they | one |
| you | they | said | one | I |
| they | I | one | you | said |
| you | said | I | one | they |

**STEP 1:** Introduce the words on letter cards.

**STEP 2:** Read words in the workbook.

**TIP:** Read down the columns as this helps students separate in memory sight words from words that letter-sounds can be used to work out (regular words). Words that can be worked out should be read across the page.

## Any mistakes?

| | | | | |
|---|---|---|---|---|
| jam | you | they | job | one |
| slug | jug | yum | slim | yum |
| clap | quit | one | scat | they |
| job | said | stem | bib | you |
| slim | drag | jam | slam | jug |
| scat | clop | slug | jog | quit |
| bib | they | clap | yet | said |
| slam | jog | slim | clop | drag |

**TIP:** Check the problem solver section of the **Teacher's Manual** for help when working with students who seem to have difficulty in making progress.

____ ____ ____ ____

1 2 3 4

Ask the students if they can figure out what the mystery word is. Write each letter in the space as they figure out what it is. Here are the clues.

**Letter 1:** Is the same as the first letter of *'Sam'*.

**Letter 2:** Is the same letter that is last letter in a word for a very fast plane. It's in **List 6** of this module.

**Letter 3:** Is the same letter as the one in the middle of *'cot'*.

**Letter 4:** Is the letter that will make the word rhyme with *'hop'*.

What is the mystery word?

**TIP:** The aim of this activity is to encourage students to think about words and letters. It also encourages students to learn how to listen to language and to respond to it with actions. The activity requires students to take a set of simple verbal instructions and implement them.

Read the clues to the students one at a time. Try to ensure that students think about the sounds that words make. For example, they should think of the first sound in the word *'Sam'*, rather than thinking about how *'Sam'* is written.

The ability to think through and act on verbal information is important for the development of high-level thinking. Give students as much help as they need to be able to complete this activity successfully. It may be difficult for some students to think through all the steps they need to execute. Give them as much assistance as they need. The activity should be challenging but lots of fun.

Teachers can invent other code puzzles in which students have to think through a set of verbal instructions to work out a message or words.

Criteria for time trials to progress to the next list in **Module 2** is 38 words in 45 seconds.

# MODULE 3

## More Initial Blends

# Overview of Module 3

| Section | Words | Letters introduced | | Letters used | |
|---|---|---|---|---|---|
| | | Consonants | | Vowels | Consonants |
| | | Initial | Final | | |
| List 1 | fan<br>dud<br>brag<br>kit<br>gum<br>nap<br>tub<br>hen | br | _n | a e i u | f k h d t g p n<br>m b<br>br |
| List 2 | quip<br>stub<br>snap<br>jig<br>bug<br>yam<br>hem<br>dab | sn | | a e i u | j y h b p g<br>m d<br>st sn qu |
| List 3 | snub<br>wig<br>pram<br>van<br>stun<br>prod<br>jot<br>trap | v pr | | a i o u | w v j b g m n d<br>t p<br>sn pr st tr |
| Review 1 | fan snub<br>quip wig<br>kit pram<br>stub bug<br>van nap<br>jig trap<br>stun brag<br>yam jot<br>vat snap | | | | |
| List 4 | snug<br>bud<br>grub<br>rob<br>trim<br>pan<br>fib<br>bin | gr | | a i o u | r p f b g d m n<br>sn gr tr |
| List 5 | vet<br>grab<br>dam<br>him<br>drum<br>snip<br>glum<br>mob | gl | | a e i o u | v d h m t b p<br>gr dr sn gl |

| Section | Words | Letters introduced | | Letters used | |
|---|---|---|---|---|---|
| | | Consonants | | Vowels | Consonants |
| | | Initial | Final | | |
| List 6 | shed<br>scab<br>plod<br>bub<br>snag<br>plug<br>win<br>step | sh pl | | a e i o u | w b d g n p<br>sh sc pl sn st |
| Review 2 | bud grab<br>snip trim<br>snag dam<br>vet win<br>yam scab<br>plod drum<br>glum mob<br>grub quip<br>shed plug<br>stun bub | | | | |
| List 7 | cub<br>shop<br>grin<br>fox<br>spot<br>six<br>bid<br>scud | sp | _x | i o u | c f s b p n x t d<br>sh gr sp sc |
| List 8 | wax<br>shun<br>tram<br>chin<br>frog<br>span<br>cob<br>hug | ch fr | | a i o u | w c h x m n g b<br>sh ch tr fr sp |
| List 9 | spin<br>box<br>thin<br>club<br>bus<br>ship<br>chop<br>from | th | | i o u | b x s p m n<br>th sh ch sp cl fr |
| List 10 | Unusual words<br>me<br>we<br>he<br>she<br>be | | | e | m w h b<br>sh |
| Review 3 | frog spin<br>box wig<br>chop vet<br>ship from<br>scat she<br>fox trim<br>club van<br>shun prod<br>wax let<br>chin snag<br>we be | | | | |

| | | | | | |
|---|---|---|---|---|---|
| fan | dud | brag | kit | nap | kit |
| hen | brag | tub | nap | gum | dud |
| tub | kit | hen | brag | dud | gum |
| nap | gum | fan | tub | hen | nap |
| gum | nap | tub | gum | kit | brag |
| kit | dud | nap | hen | brag | fan |
| brag | hen | kit | fan | tub | gum |
| fan | nap | brag | tub | kit | hen |

Letters introduced in this list: **br _n**

All letters used in this list: **a e i u br f k h d t g p n m b d**

**TIP:** Remember to use the large letter cards to help teach students how to use letter-sounds to work out words. First introduce the new letters, then make each word with the letters and work with the students to blend the sounds together to make the word. Be careful to only use letter-sounds not letter-names.

## Any mistakes?

| | | | | | |
|---|---|---|---|---|---|
| bug | stub | quip | jig | snap | yam |
| hem | dab | yam | bug | stub | quip |
| yam | bug | bad | stub | quip | snap |
| quip | stub | hem | dab | jig | snap |
| jig | quip | bug | jig | snap | dab |
| yam | jig | stub | snap | bug | hem |
| dab | snap | quip | hem | yam | jig |
| quip | yam | jig | bug | hem | stub |

Letters introduced in this list: **sn**

All letters used in this list: **a e i u  st sn qu j b y h p g m d**

**TIP:** Students may not know the meaning of some of the words they are decoding. Explaining the meaning of words is one useful way to enhance their vocabularies, however, the focus of decoding skills activities should not be on understanding the meaning of words. It is when students can employ their decoding skills to read text that comprehension is important. Building effective decoding skills will, in the long-term, enhance students' comprehension.

## Any mistakes?

| | | | | | |
|---|---|---|---|---|---|
| wig | pram | trap | jot | snub | van |
| snub | wig | pram | van | jot | wig |
| pram | snub | van | prod | wig | jot |
| van | stun | prod | wig | trap | snub |
| stun | van | jot | trap | prod | pram |
| prod | jot | stun | snub | van | trap |
| jot | trap | wig | pram | stun | prod |
| trap | jot | snub | stun | pram | stun |

Letters introduced in this list: **v pr**
All letters used in this list: **a i o u sn pr st tr w v j b g m n d t p**

## Any mistakes?

| | | | | | |
|---|---|---|---|---|---|
| fan | trap | brag | van | wig | bad |
| quip | nap | jot | jig | snub | snap |
| kit | bug | snap | stun | fan | jot |
| stub | pram | bad | yam | vat | brag |
| van | wig | fan | trap | brag | quip |
| jig | snub | quip | nap | jot | vat |
| stun | stub | kit | bug | snap | quip |
| yam | vat | stub | pram | bad | snub |

| | | | | | | | | | |
|---|---|---|---|---|---|---|---|---|---|
| b | p | e | p | a | t | v | w | i | g |
| t | r | a | p | s | n | a | p | m | u |
| h | a | m | s | t | u | n | r | q | m |
| k | m | u | g | u | m | h | o | u | u |
| s | s | t | u | b | a | e | d | i | g |
| l | h | i | m | u | s | n | u | b | o |
| j | m | w | i | g | u | m | d | r | q |
| t | r | a | p | o | d | m | v | a | u |
| u | p | r | o | d | e | h | e | m | i |
| b | r | a | g | h | e | n | s | i | p |

**brag van snap stub wig tub trap**

**gum quip snub pram prod hem hen**

Ask the students to find the words above. They can colour each letter square that is part of a word in the puzzle. Words could be coloured a different colour. Then they can see if they can find any other words. Words are arranged horizontally (across), vertically (down) or diagonally.

| | | | | | |
|---|---|---|---|---|---|
| snug | bin | rob | trim | pan | fib |
| bud | pan | bin | rob | fib | grub |
| rob | trim | snug | grub | bin | pan |
| grub | fib | bud | rob | snug | pan |
| trim | rob | bun | snug | grub | bin |
| pan | grub | fib | bin | bud | trim |
| fib | bud | pan | fib | rob | snug |
| bin | snug | grub | pan | trim | bud |

Letters introduced in this list: **gr**

All letters used in this list: **a i o u sn gr tr r p f b g m n d**

## Any mistakes?

| | | | | | |
|---|---|---|---|---|---|
| vet | grab | dam | drum | him | snip |
| grab | dam | him | snip | drum | glum |
| dam | him | drum | vet | snip | mob |
| him | drum | snip | mob | glum | vet |
| drum | snip | glum | vet | mob | grab |
| snip | glum | mob | grab | vet | dam |
| glum | mob | vet | dam | grab | him |
| mob | vet | grab | him | dam | drum |

Letters introduced in this list: **gl**

All letters used in this list: **a e i o u gr dr sn gl v d h m p b t**

## Any mistakes?

| | | | | | |
|---|---|---|---|---|---|
| shed | bub | scab | snag | plod | plug |
| scab | snag | plod | plug | bub | win |
| plod | plug | bub | win | snag | step |
| bub | win | snag | step | plug | shed |
| snag | step | plug | shed | win | scab |
| plug | shed | win | scab | step | plod |
| win | scab | step | plod | shed | bub |
| step | plod | shed | bub | scab | snag |

Letters introduced in this list: **sh pl**
All letters used in this list: **a e i o u  sh sc pl sn st w b d g n p b**

## Any mistakes?

| | | | | | |
|---|---|---|---|---|---|
| bud | shed | mob | bub | dam | grab |
| snip | stun | quip | plod | win | vet |
| snag | grab | plug | glum | scab | quip |
| vet | trim | bub | grub | drum | stun |
| yam | dam | snip | shed | yam | glum |
| plod | win | snag | stun | quip | shed |
| glum | scab | vet | grab | plug | snag |
| grub | drum | yam | trim | bub | snip |

fan

hen

bug

wig

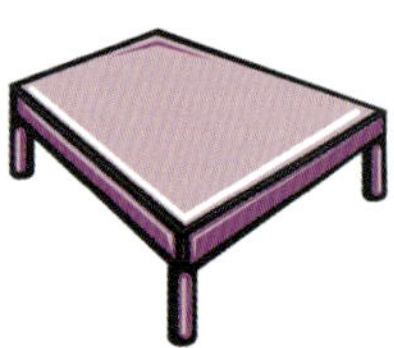

Ask students to read the first word ('**fan**') and name the first two pictures ('**man**' '**kitten**'). They should draw a line between the word '**fan**' and the picture that rhymes with '**fan**'. Repeat these steps for the other words. Pictures are of **man, kitten; dog, pen; frog, jug; pig, table.**

| | | | | | |
|---|---|---|---|---|---|
| cub | spot | bid | fox | grin | six |
| bid | fox | six | grin | shop | spot |
| six | grin | spot | shop | cub | fox |
| spot | shop | fox | cub | scud | grin |
| fox | cub | grin | scud | bid | shop |
| grin | scud | shop | bid | six | cub |
| shop | bid | cub | six | spot | scud |
| cub | six | scud | spot | fox | bid |

Letters introduced in this list: **sp _x**
All letters used in this list: **i o u sh gr sp sc c f s b p n x d t**

## Any mistakes?

wax tram shun frog chin span

shun chin tram span frog cob

tram frog chin cob span hug

chin span frog hug cob wax

frog cob span wax hug shun

span hug cob shun wax tram

cob wax hug tram shun chin

hug shun wax chin tram frog

Letters introduced in this list: **ch fr**

All letters used in this list: **a i o u sh ch tr fr sp w c h x m n b g**

**TIP:** Remember that it is essential that students master each word in the list. Make sure they reach criterion on the mastery test before progressing to the next list. Check the **Teacher's Manual** for tips on working with students who have difficulty in making progress.

## Any mistakes?

| | | | | | |
|---|---|---|---|---|---|
| spin | thin | bus | box | club | ship |
| box | club | ship | thin | bus | chop |
| thin | bus | chop | club | ship | from |
| club | ship | from | bus | chop | spin |
| bus | chop | spin | ship | from | box |
| ship | from | box | chop | spin | thin |
| chop | spin | thin | from | box | club |
| from | box | club | spin | thin | bus |

Letters introduced in this list: **th**
All letters used in this list: **i o u th sh ch sp cl fr b p x s m n**

## Any mistakes?

# Congratulations!

You have reached **LIST 10** of
**Module 3** of **LINK – Decoding**

# MODULE 3 LIST 10: Unusual words

**NOTE 1:** The program uses the term 'unusual words' to refer to words that look as if they could be read using the letter-sound rules, however, they do not obey these rules. They are presented in word families to assist students to remember that these words do not follow the normal rules. Explain carefully that these words are very tricky and must be remembered. Unusual words are slightly different from sight words. Sight words are clearly exceptions to the rules. Unusual words look as if they could be worked out, however, they do not follow the regular rules.

**NOTE 2:** Modify the lesson plan for unusual words. Make the first word '**me**'. After students have read it and used it in a sentence, leave the '**e**' displayed and substitute '**w**' for '**m**'. All other steps in the lesson remain the same.

**TIP:** Read down the columns. This helps students separate in memory unusual words from words that letter-sounds can be used to work out (regular words). Words that can be worked out should be read across the page.

| | | | | | |
|---|---|---|---|---|---|
| me | we | he | we | be | he |
| we | be | she | he | me | we |
| we | me | she | he | he | me |
| he | she | be | we | be | she |
| we | she | he | be | me | me |
| he | be | we | me | be | he |
| she | he | be | she | me | he |
| be | we | me | she | we | be |

No new letters introduced in this list.
All letters used in this list: **e** **sh b m w h**

## Any mistakes?

| | | | | | |
|---|---|---|---|---|---|
| frog | wax | trim | chop | spin | prod |
| box | chin | van | ship | wig | let |
| chop | spin | prod | scat | vet | snag |
| ship | wig | let | snag | from | we |
| scat | vet | snag | club | she | be |
| snag | from | we | shun | fox | box |
| club | she | be | wax | trim | chop |
| shun | fox | box | chin | van | ship |

_____ _____ _____

1 2 3

Ask the students if they can figure out what the mystery word is. They should write each letter in the space as they figure out what it is. Here are the clues:

**Letter 1:** Is the same as the first letter of *'frog'*.

**Letter 2:** Is the same letter that is the middle letter in a word for what a horse can do. It's in **List 1** of **Module 2**.

**Letter 3:** Makes the word rhyme with *'box'*.

What is the mystery word?

**TIP:** The aim of this activity is to encourage students to think about words and letters. It also encourages students to learn how to listen to language and to respond to it with actions. It requires students to take a set of simple verbal instructions and implement them.

Read the clues to the students one at a time. Try to ensure that students think about the sounds that words make. For example, they should think of the first sound in the word *'frog'*. To do this they will need to segment the blend *'fr'*.

The ability to think through and act on verbal information is important for the development of high-level thinking. Give students as much help as they need to be able to complete this activity successfully. It may be difficult for some students to think through all the steps they need to execute. Give them as much assistance as they need. The activity should be challenging but lots of fun.

Teachers can invent other code puzzles where students have to think through a set of verbal instructions to work out a message or word.

Criteria for time trials to progress to the next list in **Module 3** is 38 words in 45 seconds.

# MODULE 4

## Introducing Final Consonant Digraphs

# Overview of Module 4

| Section | Words | Letters introduced | | Letters used | |
|---|---|---|---|---|---|
| | | Consonants | | Vowels | Consonants |
| | | Initial | Final | | |
| List 1 | sack<br>fled<br>neck<br>flip<br>truck<br>chum<br>sock<br>slid<br>lick<br>when | wh fl | _ck | a e i o u | s n l d p m n<br>wh fl tr ch sl ck |
| List 2 | tell<br>quick<br>fill<br>whip<br>mix<br>doll<br>struck<br>gull<br>strip<br>quack | str | _ll | a e i o u | t f m d g p x<br>qu wh ll ck<br>str |
| List 3 | crack<br>cram<br>smell<br>quill<br>frock<br>slab<br>dull<br>brick<br>luck<br>plus | cr sm | | a e i o u | d l m b s<br>qu cr sm fr sl br<br>pl ck ll |
| Review 1 | van chum<br>flip truck<br>when crack<br>tell quick<br>whip doll<br>struck gull<br>strip quack<br>speck quill<br>frock slab<br>dull quip | | | | |
| List 4 | lass<br>black<br>jell<br>mess<br>check<br>kiss<br>grill<br>moss<br>kick<br>fuss | bl | _ss | a e i o u | l j m k f<br>ch bl gr ss ck ll |

| Section | Words | Letters introduced | | Letters used | |
|---|---|---|---|---|---|
| | | Consonants | | Vowels | Consonants |
| | | Initial | Final | | |
| List 5 | smell<br>mass<br>swell<br>whack<br>less<br>smock<br>hull<br>hiss<br>chill<br>pluck | sw | | a e i o u | m l h<br>wh sm sw ch<br>pl ss ll ck |
| List 6 | skull<br>yuck<br>miss<br>track<br>quell<br>toss<br>deck<br>spill<br>stuck<br>shock | sk | | a e i o u | y m t d<br>qu th sh sk tr sp st<br>ll ck ss |
| Review 2 | wax shock<br>lass jell<br>mess check<br>grill moss<br>mass whack<br>swell skull<br>yuck quell<br>toss spill | | | | |
| List 7 | slack<br>cash<br>blob<br>skip<br>swam<br>fresh<br>tax<br>trick<br>wish<br>crush | | | a e i o u | c t w p b m x<br>sl bl sk sw fr tr<br>cr ck sh |
| List 8 | twin<br>slash<br>pick<br>bliss<br>flesh<br>chock<br>swish<br>bell<br>gosh<br>rush | tw | | a e i o u | p b g r n<br>ch tw sl bl fl sw sh<br>ck ss ll |

| Section | Words | Letters introduced | | Letters used | |
|---|---|---|---|---|---|
| | | Consonants | | Vowels | Consonants |
| | | Initial | Final | | |
| List 9 | Unusual words<br>_all<br>ball<br>call<br>fall<br>small<br>hall<br>wall<br>stall<br>tall<br>squall | squ | _all | | b c f h w t<br>squ sm st all |
| List 10 | Sight words<br>do<br>to<br>our<br>please<br>are<br>very | | | | |
| Review 3 | hall cash<br>fresh fall<br>stall slash<br>swish bell<br>slack gosh<br>small tax<br>please rush<br>wall squall<br>our crush | | | | |

| | | | | | |
|---|---|---|---|---|---|
| sack | flip | fled | chum | neck | truck |
| fled | truck | neck | sock | flip | chum |
| neck | chum | flip | slid | truck | sock |
| flip | sock | truck | lick | chum | slid |
| truck | slid | chum | when | sock | lick |
| chum | lick | sock | sack | slid | when |
| sock | when | slid | fled | lick | sack |
| slid | sack | lick | neck | when | fled |
| lick | fled | when | flip | sack | neck |
| when | neck | sack | truck | fled | flip |

Letters introduced in this list: **wh fl _ck**

All letters used in this list: **a e i o u ch wh fl tr sl s n l d p m n ck**

**NOTE 1:** This module introduces consonant digraphs. Tell students that digraphs are two letters that work together to make one sound. In this list '**wh**' and '**ck**' are digraphs. Talk about the letters that make the '**kkk**' sounds. In some words this is '**c**' ('**cat**'), in others it's '**k**' ('**kit**'). When the '**kkk**' sound occurs at the end of a word, it is usually spelled '**ck**'.

## Any mistakes?

| | | | | |
|---|---|---|---|---|
| tell | fill | struck | mix | strip |
| quick | whip | gull | doll | quack |
| fill | mix | strip | struck | tell |
| whip | doll | quack | gull | quick |
| mix | struck | tell | strip | whip |
| doll | gull | quick | quack | fill |
| struck | strip | whip | tell | doll |
| gull | quack | fill | quick | mix |
| strip | tell | doll | whip | gull |
| quack | quick | mix | fill | struck |

Letters introduced in this list: **str _ll**

All letters used in this list: **a e i o u qu wh str t f m d g p x ll ck**

**TIP:** Remember to complete the time trial at the end of this module. Students should reach the criterion before continuing on to the next list.

## Any mistakes?

| | | | | | |
|---|---|---|---|---|---|
| crack | frock | dull | luck | cram | smell |
| cram | slab | brick | plus | quill | quill |
| smell | dull | luck | cram | frock | frock |
| quill | brick | plus | quill | smell | slab |
| frock | luck | cram | frock | crack | dull |
| slab | plus | quill | smell | slab | brick |
| dull | cram | frock | crack | brick | luck |
| brick | crack | smell | slab | dull | plus |
| luck | quill | crack | brick | plus | cram |
| plus | smell | slab | dull | luck | crack |

Letters introduced in this list: **cr sm**

All letters used in this list: **a e i o u qu cr sm fr sl br pl d l m b s ck ll**

**TIP:** As the number of letters increases, some students may have difficulty. It is essential that every student masters each list before progressing. Read the **Problem Solver** section of the **Teacher's Manual** for ideas on how to assist students who are encountering difficulty.

## Any mistakes?

| | | | | |
|---|---|---|---|---|
| quip | van | when | whip | quack |
| flip | quill | tell | struck | gull |
| when | quack | whip | van | slab |
| tell | gull | struck | frock | quick |
| whip | slab | flip | strip | doll |
| struck | quick | frock | dull | crack |
| when | doll | strip | flip | truck |
| frock | crack | dull | quip | chum |
| strip | truck | flip | when | quill |
| dull | chum | quip | tell | van |

| | | | | | | | | | |
|---|---|---|---|---|---|---|---|---|---|
| p | v | a | n | f | l | e | d | m | p |
| l | x | s | m | q | u | i | c | k | a |
| u | z | t | r | i | c | k | h | i | d |
| s | t | r | u | c | k | i | k | d | o |
| n | m | i | x | m | c | r | u | s | h |
| s | a | p | a | t | h | e | y | e | s |
| c | h | e | c | k | i | d | u | l | l |
| h | i | t | l | t | d | o | g | l | u |
| i | m | m | o | w | a | l | l | x | c |
| p | s | a | d | o | b | l | o | c | k |

**dull struck van quick fled plus strip**
**mix luck check him crush block**

Ask the students if they can find the words above. They can colour each letter square that is part of a word in the puzzle. Words could be coloured a different colour. See if they can find any other words. Words are arranged horizontally (across), vertically (down) or diagonally. There are 36 words altogether.

**TIP:** Some letters may be used in more than one word.

| | | | | |
|---|---|---|---|---|
| lass | jell | mess | black | moss |
| black | check | kiss | jell | check |
| jell | kiss | moss | mess | fuss |
| mess | grill | fuss | check | lass |
| check | moss | lass | kiss | black |
| kiss | fuss | jell | grill | mess |
| grill | black | check | moss | jell |
| moss | lass | grill | kick | fuss |
| kick | mess | kick | fuss | grill |
| fuss | kick | black | lass | kick |

Letters introduced in this list: **bl _ss**

All letters used in this list: **a e i o u ch bl gr l j m k f ll ss ck**

**NOTE:** Tell students that we've seen some words that end in the sound 'sss'. Ask them if they can think of a word. 'Bus' is a word that ends in the sound 'sss'. Explain that there is another way of writing words that end in the sound 'sss'. Many words end in 'ss'; in fact, (except for the case of plurals), most words end in 'ss'. This list contains some of them.

## Any mistakes?

| | | | | |
|---|---|---|---|---|
| smell | swell | smock | whack | mass |
| mass | whack | hull | less | swell |
| swell | less | hiss | smock | whack |
| whack | smock | chill | hull | less |
| less | hull | pluck | hiss | smock |
| smock | hiss | smell | chill | hull |
| hull | chill | mass | pluck | hiss |
| hiss | pluck | swell | smell | chill |
| chill | smell | whack | mass | pluck |
| pluck | mass | less | swell | smell |

Letters introduced in this list: **sw**

All letters used in this list: **a e i o u  wh ch sm sw pl m l h ss ll ck**

**TIP:** Some words in the list are very similar (e.g., '**smell**' and '**swell**'). Research indicates that when decoding, good readers analyse every letter of the word. **Reading LINK – Decoding** is designed to facilitate students' ability to focus on every letter in sequence. Ensure that students do not make 'careless' errors by guessing. They must be absolutely accurate on every word they read.

## Any mistakes?

| | | | | | |
|---|---|---|---|---|---|
| yuck | miss | quell | track | toss | skull |
| miss | skull | toss | quell | deck | track |
| skull | track | deck | toss | spill | quell |
| track | quell | spill | deck | stuck | toss |
| quell | toss | stuck | spill | shock | deck |
| toss | deck | shock | stuck | yuck | spill |
| deck | spill | yuck | shock | miss | stuck |
| spill | stuck | miss | yuck | skull | shock |
| stuck | shock | skull | miss | track | yuck |
| shock | yuck | track | skull | quell | miss |

Letters introduced in this list: **sk**

All letters used in this list: **a e i o u qu th sh st sk tr sp y m t d ll ck ss**

**TIP:** Many lists contain words that students may not understand (e.g., '**quell**'). Use this as an opportunity to increase students' vocabularies by explaining the meaning of all words.

## Any mistakes?

| | | | | |
|---|---|---|---|---|
| wax | thick | smell | check | moss |
| wax | toss | jell | whack | whack |
| jell | yuck | moss | wax | skull |
| check | swell | skull | quell | quell |
| moss | mass | spill | shock | spill |
| whack | grill | thick | toss | shock |
| skull | fuss | yuck | swell | thick |
| quell | smell | mass | grill | toss |
| spill | mess | fuss | mess | yuck |
| shock | lass | wax | smell | swell |

1. Is that a _ _ _ _ of dust on the little red bag?

2. We went to the vet with the _ _ _. He is sick. Will the vet fix _ _ _ do you think?

3. "Yuck. This is a _ _ _ _," said Mum. "Fix it up."

4. If you run, you will slip in the mud. You will _ _ _ wet. Mum will be _ _ _.

**get neck go mess check think**
**mad speck sock cat him shock**

Ask students if they can think of the words to complete each sentence. Some of the words listed below the sentences can be used but some will not fit. Students are also correct if they can come up with words that fit with the sense of the sentence but are not on the list.

| | | | | |
|---|---|---|---|---|
| slack | wish | swam | cash | tax |
| cash | crush | fresh | slack | trick |
| blob | cash | tax | skip | wish |
| skip | slack | trick | blob | crush |
| swam | skip | wish | fresh | cash |
| fresh | blob | crush | swam | slack |
| tax | fresh | cash | trick | skip |
| trick | swam | slack | tax | blob |
| wish | trick | skip | crush | fresh |
| crush | tax | blob | wish | swam |

No new letters introduced in this list.

All letters used in this list: **a e i o u sl bl sk sw fr tr cr c t w p b m x ck sh**

**TIP:** Even if students have difficulty in grasping the meaning of some words, it is important that they can work out (decode) what the word says. If they have strong decoding skills, their ability to understand written text will be dramatically improved.

## Any mistakes?

| | | | | | |
|---|---|---|---|---|---|
| twin | bell | pick | slash | flesh | rush |
| slash | gosh | bliss | twin | swish | chock |
| pick | rush | flesh | bliss | bell | slash |
| bliss | chock | swish | pick | gosh | twin |
| flesh | slash | bell | swish | rush | bliss |
| swish | twin | gosh | flesh | chock | pick |
| bell | bliss | rush | gosh | slash | swish |
| gosh | pick | chock | bell | twin | flesh |
| rush | swish | slash | chock | bliss | gosh |
| chock | flesh | twin | rush | pick | bell |

Letters introduced in this list: **tw**
All letters used in this list: **a e i o u ch tw sl bl fl sw p b g r n ck ss ll sh**

## Any mistakes?

# You are a super reader!

You have reached **List 9** of
**Module 4** of **LINK – Decoding**

# MODULE 4 LIST 9: Unusual words – _all

**NOTE:** 'Unusual' words are those that look as if they should be able to be decoded using letter-sound correspondences, however, they do not follow the regular rules. They need to be learnt as a pattern that has an unusual sound structure. This is slightly different from sight words that are distinctive and need to be learnt as individual whole words. Words that have been identified in the program as 'unusual words' are a group of words sharing an unusual pattern. Students need to learn the pattern.

Tell the students that these 'unusual' words can be tricky. They look like they can be sounded out, just like other words, but they have a strange sound. They don't follow the rules. We have to remember them specially.

To help students store these words in a distinctive memory structure they can be read down the page.

Modify the lesson plan for unusual words. When making the words with letter cards, the first word '**ball**' can be made. After students have read it and used it in a sentence, leave the '**all**' displayed and substitute '**c**' for '**b**'. All other steps in the lesson remain the same.

| | | | | |
|---|---|---|---|---|
| ball | hall | squall | fall | call |
| call | wall | ball | small | fall |
| fall | stall | call | hall | small |
| small | tall | fall | wall | hall |
| hall | squall | small | stall | wall |
| wall | ball | hall | tall | stall |
| stall | call | wall | squall | tall |
| tall | fall | stall | ball | squall |
| squall | small | tall | call | stall |
| ball | hall | squall | fall | small |

Letters introduced in this list: **squ _all**
All letters used in this list: **sm st squ b c f h w t all**

## Any mistakes?

| | | | | |
|---|---|---|---|---|
| to | do | our | are | very |
| do | very | are | please | are |
| please | to | do | our | are |
| do | are | very | very | to |
| very | to | our | our | do |
| do | our | are | do | our |
| are | to | do | please | to |
| do | are | please | to | very |
| do | please | very | our | do |
| very | our | do | are | please |

**TIP:** Read down the columns. This helps students separate in memory sight words from words that letter-sounds can be used to work out (regular words). Words that can be worked out should be read across the page.

## Any mistakes?

| | | | | |
|---|---|---|---|---|
| hall | tax | want | slack | fall |
| fresh | gosh | wall | small | cash |
| stall | bell | squall | please | our |
| swish | slash | crush | rush | to |
| slack | fall | hall | tax | wall |
| small | cash | fresh | gosh | squall |
| please | our | stall | bell | crush |
| rush | to | swish | slash | hall |
| to | swish | hall | rush | please |
| fall | small | want | gosh | wall |

# My Pet

My pet is little. I call him Ben. Dad calls him Big Ben.

I can hug my pet. I can run with my pet. He runs and jumps in the mud. I run but I do not go in the mud.

When we run, he has a nap. Then I can pat him and hug him and I can kiss him. Mum said not to kiss him, but I do.

Dad said that he will get big. He will get big and fat and he will smell bad. Then I will not hug him. And if he smells bad, I will not kiss him.

What is my pet?

He is not a little dog.
He is not a cat. He is not a fox. He is not a small rat.

My pet is a small ___ ___ ___.

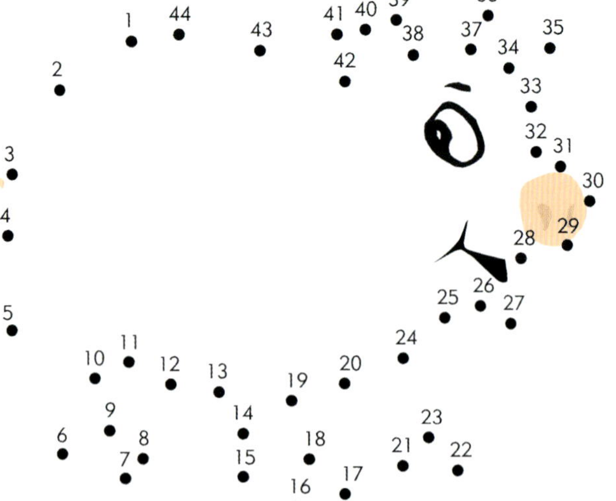

**TIP:** The aim of this activity is to give students an opportunity to use their decoding skills to read text. The activity should be fun and enjoyable. They should be able to decode all the words in the text with ease.

Encourage students to focus on the ideas in the text. Help them to use the clues to work out what the pet could be. For example, it's small, so it could be a puppy or kitten, but it says that it's not a dog or cat. It likes the mud. What kind of animal likes to roll in the mud?

When students have read the text, talked about all the clues, and guessed what the pet could be, they can complete the dot-to-dot drawing and write the kind of pet on the lines.

For each list of words, read the words in the workbook. When the students are ready, see how many words they can read in 45 seconds. Write the number of the list in the last row. Students can mark and colour the number of words they read on the graph. Students may take a time trial on each list as many times as necessary. The goal of each time trial is for the student to read one more word than they did in the previous time trial. Criterion to progress to the next list of words is marked on the graph – 40 words in 45 seconds. When students reach criterion, they should receive a reward. Public recognition for achievement is a powerful reward; for example, as students reach criterion, they could stand while the class applauds them.

# READING LINK

## Workbook 1

# *Award of Completion*

The following student has successfully completed all requirements for this award.

______________________________

Signed ____________________ Date __________

KNOWLEDGE BOOKS AND SOFTWARE PUBLISHING